THE TEXAS HILL COUNTRY

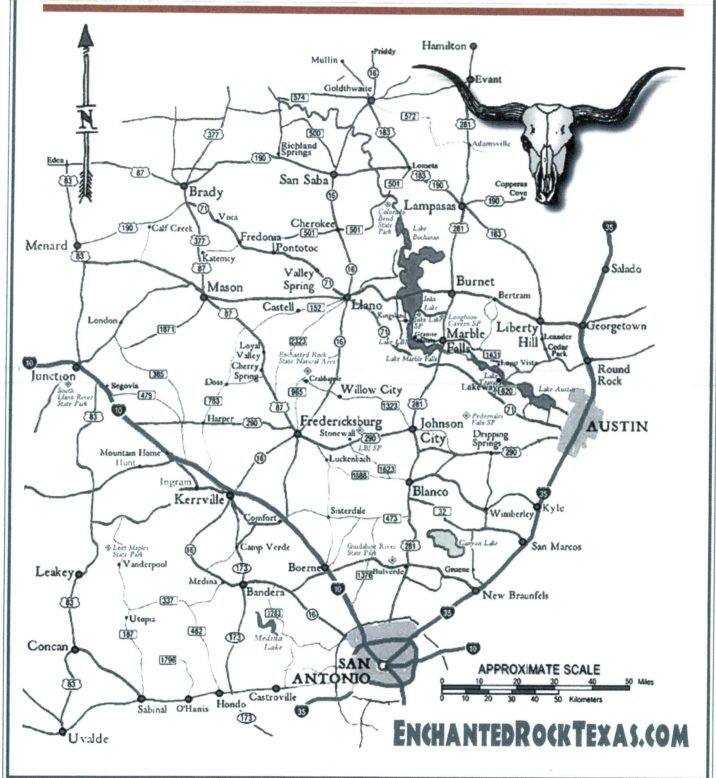

ENCHANTEDROCKTEXAS.COM

To order additional copies of this book, contact:
Xlibris
844-714-8691
www.Xlibris.com
Orders@Xlibris.com

ISBN: Softcover   978-1-4568-1878-4
         EBook   978-1-4771-6109-8

Library of Congress Control Number: 2010917891

Print information available on the last page

Rev. date: 06/08/2021

THE HISTORY OF
ENCHANTED ROCK
IN THE TEXAS HILL COUNTRY
WRITTEN & ILLUSTRATED BY
IRA KENNEDY

This is the place where Texas began.
Enchanted Rock is part of the basement
or bedrock structure of Texas.
Around this core, the rest of the state slowly formed.
The foundation is stable, it is hard, and it is ancient.

--Interpretative Exhibit
Enchanted Rock State Natural Area

EnchantedRockTexas.com

We are the longing of our ancestors.
We are their dream.
Through us they dream themselves awake.

--I.K.

Dedicated to my sons David, Brian & Kevin
and to their dreams.

CONTENTS

ILLUSTRATIONS

PREFACE

Enchanted Rock is Central Texas' most intriguing and enigmatic natural landmark. Rising from the surrounding oak savanna amid a chain of rugged granite hills, the massive dome rises 325 feet from base to summit and covers an area of one square mile. Approached from the south one is offered a sudden and spectacular panorama of this remarkable attraction.

I first encountered Enchanted Rock in 1962. Gradually, I was captivated by its incredible beauty and inherent mystery. In the early 1970s I camped there frequently, often alone, well past the reach of civilization. I became intimately familiar with its creeks, its caves, and its granite outcrops, from Sandy Creek to Walnut Spring Creek and beyond. In the winter I cracked ice-covered springs for water, and later in the season noted which ones survived a summer drought. In the process I learned much about the land and myself as well, but the full meaning and history of the place remained elusive.

Eventually, I turned to a wide variety of books on Texas history to fill in the gaps of my knowledge. I soon realized there was more to the place than a series of facts and events presented in chronological order.

What was known of Enchanted Rock prior to the seventeenth century is lost to history. To reach into its prehistory I delved into hundreds of books on Native Americans, anthropology, archaeology, and mythology. Gradually, like photographic paper in a developing tray, a remarkably detailed image began to emerge.

When humans find a place new to them, they cast a longing gaze across the landscape and see, as in a still pond, not the land itself but a reflection of their innermost desires. Due to its unusual shape, it was seen by the Native Americans as a place set apart by the Creator as a religious shrine. Later, with the arrival of the Spanish and subsequently the Texans, its mineral-rich substance, particularly the deposits of gold and silver, became its primary attraction.

Today, over 350,000 people annually come from towns, cities, states, and foreign countries for rest and recreation at Enchanted Rock.

While the emphasis on the use of Enchanted Rock has changed, its original purpose is still intact. To this day Native Americans journey to this landmark for prayer and ceremony as do many people of other races and religions.

Enchanted Rock inspires awe and reverence. There is a sense of being, of presence inherent to this unique monolith which is apparent even today. That will never change.

INTRODUCTION

Sparsely scattered across the continent are monuments, natural in origin. Some are beautiful, others bizarre; a few reach deeper than the eye or the mind to touch the human psyche. They are named holy. Enchanted Rock, which rises above the surrounding oak savanna like a megalithic monument is such a place.

Composed of some of the oldest rock on earth, this ancient landmark began taking shape more than a billion years ago. From the earth's core, underground rivers of magma (molten rock) rose like mushrooms that cooled into rock before they surfaced. Cataclysmic changes occurred. Great mountains and oceans rose and fell. Volcanoes thrust skyward. Rampaging storms deluged the land. Massive rivers formed and slowly subsided, creating the deep canyons and valleys of the Texas Hill Country.

Over the millennia, erosion worked its way down to the old rock. Finally, some 10 million years ago, Enchanted Rock emerged, eventually to stand 1,845 feet above sea level and 325 feet from base to summit, and one square mile in area. It is the second largest granite dome in the United States —the largest being Stone Mountain in Georgia.

Enchanted Rock is the geologic center of Texas. From almost any place in the park you can see examples representing the whole evolution of plant life—from lichen (the slowest growing plant on earth) to mosses, to ferns, to herbaceous plants, to shrubs and finally trees.

Within the park's 1,643 acres are over five hundred species of plants. Over one hundred of these inhabit the vernal pools, weathered pits which impound soil and water on the summit of Enchanted Rock and the surrounding outcrops. The vernal pools are delicate ecosystems, supporting a unique invertebrate, the fairy shrimp.

Whether the pools appear as bare rock depressions or filled with plant life, all the pools are in a process of evolution which has required thousands of years. Avoid walking through or otherwise disturbing these areas. In their dormant state, the fairy shrimp appear as dust when the pools are dry. Almost a dozen of the native plants are unique to the area. The Hammock fern, *Blechnum occidentale* L.: the Basin bellflower, *Campanula reverchonii*; and Rock quillwort, *Isoetes lithophylla*, can be found here, all of which are considered either threatened or endangered by the Smithsonian Institution

Geologically Enchanted Rock and the adjacent granite domes called *inselbergs*—island mountains—contain amethyst, beryl, fluorite, pink feldspar, gold, silver, topaz, tourmaline, and veins of crystalline quartz. The exposed surface of Enchanted Rock is but a small portion of the Enchanted Rock *batholith*, the upward intrusion of granite, which occupies over one hundred square miles beneath the earth's surface. The surrounding area is variously called the Llano Uplift, the Granite Highlands, or the Central Mineral Region.

Along the northwest face of Enchanted Rock, near the summit is Enchanted Rock Cave. Actually a capped crevice over 600 feet long with some 20 entrances, it is one of the largest caves formed within an inselberg mass. Although exploration of the cave is permitted, it should not be done without adequate equipment. The absolute darkness and vertical drops near the lower levels of the cave make it very hazardous for amateurs. Formerly the nesting place for rock and canyon wrens, and a roosting site for cave myotis and other bats, Enchanted Rock Cave is one of the park's most ecologically damaged areas .

Bedrock metates, one of the few Indian artifacts on view at Enchanted Rock State Natural Area, can be located between Freshman Mountain and Buzzards Roost near the creekbed. The metates along with stone monos were used to grind seeds. The metates are identified by the concave depressions on granite boulders which are, as a result of years of use, polished smooth.

Here, around twelve thousand years ago, our story begins.

THE FIRST PEOPLE

*Hunting the mastodon and mammoth, the first people of America wandered out of ice and tundra into the New World.
One of their migrations charted the Old Pinta Trail, which became a well-worn route that stretched from Canada down the Great Plains, crossed Sandy Creek at Enchanted Rock, and continued to South Texas.*

These hunter-gatherers had flint-tipped spears, fire, and stories. With these resources, some twelve thousand years ago, the first Texans became the wellspring of Plains Indian culture. On the basis of archaeological evidence human habitation at Enchanted Rock can be traced back 10,000 years. Paleo-Indian projectile points, or arrowheads, 11-12,000 years old have been found in the area upstream and downstream from The Rock. The oldest authenticated projectile point found within the present day park is a Plainview type, dating from 8,000 B.C..

The names of the original tribes in the area are not known. The first written records, dating from the sixteenth century, are of the Tonkawa. An interesting commentary on Enchanted Rock and its inhabitants is found in *The Scouting Expedition of McCulloch's Texas Rangers*, by Samuel C. Reid, Jr., published in 1848: "We are unable to give to the reader the traditionary cause why this place was so named," Reid wrote about Enchanted Rock, "but nevertheless, the Indians had a great awe, amounting almost to a reverence for it, and would tell many legendary tales connected with it and the fate of a few

brave warriors, the last of a tribe now extinct, who defended themselves there for any years as in a strong castle, against the attacks of their hostile brethren. But they were finally overcome and totally annihilated, and ever since the 'Enchanted Rock' has been looked upon as the exclusive property of these phantom warriors. This is one of the many tales which the Indians tell concerning it."

It is very likely that Reid's informants were the Tonkawa, who frequently served as guides to the Rangers, and who, more than any other tribe, would have had any knowledge of "a tribe now extinct" that inhabited Enchanted Rock.

Due to the lack of published research, the religious beliefs of the Tonkawa are very sketchy, but seem to have been shaped in large measure by Tonkawa myths regarding the spirits of the dead. In *The Indians of Texas*, published in 1961, the author W. W. Newcomb Jr., notes: "Souls of women were thought to go directly to the home in the west singing as they went; souls of men, however, were apt to hang around watching their living relatives and calling to them. If the dead were not properly buried, their spirits would remain to haunt the miscreants.

Certain places were avoided, particularly at night, because strange sounds attributed to the souls of the dead were heard there." Possibly, some of the more ghostly legends and reports of the Indian's fearful reactions regarding Enchanted Rock and the mysterious noises said to emit from it can be traced to the Tonkawa.

In the early 1700s the Apache displaced the Tonkawa at Enchanted Rock. It is with the Apache myths, which have been the subject of greater study, that we get a more complete picture of Plains Indian beliefs as they relate to the sacred nature of Enchanted Rock.

According to the Apache, the Giver of Life sent the *Gan*, or mountain spirits, to teach the people a better way to live, govern, hunt, and cure illness. Accordingly to the myth, these benevolent but powerful mountain spirits live forever in the mountain's caves and can be appealed to for guidance and protection.

By the end of the 1700s the Comanche had displaced the Apache. To the Comanche, like many other plains tribes, the sun was the universal father.

Jean Louis Berlandier, in his firsthand account, *The Indians of Texas in 1830,* wrote: "The sun seems to be the single object of creation they venerate most assiduously... In general all the nomadic peoples make no sacrifice to him... After the sun, the earth takes second place in their devotion... Their various superstitious ceremonials, handed down generation after generation from their ancestors or picked up in some other way, are celebrated amid the majestic monuments of nature... You may see Comanches and others, hoping for a revelation or some important inspiration... seek out some high and lonely place where they build a sort of sepulchre of stones. There they pay homage to the object of their veneration, whereupon they go to sleep hoping for a dream that will reveal the counsel they have prayed for."

There is no question that Enchanted Rock was the site for both the Gan dance of the Apache and the vision quest of the Comanche and other Plains Indians. Some of the earliest European visitors mention seeing stone sepulchres on the summit. As recently as thirty years ago flint shards were found on a large flat area on the northwest summit.

In 1892, James R. Mooney wrote in *The Ghost Dance Religion*, about Wovoka, a famous Paiute prophet and

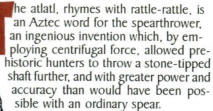

ABOUT THE ATLATL

The atlatl, rhymes with rattle-rattle, is an Aztec word for the spearthrower, an ingenious invention which, by employing centrifugal force, allowed prehistoric hunters to throw a stone-tipped shaft further, and with greater power and accuracy than would have been possible with an ordinary spear.

The main shaft, made of a pithy-centered lightweight wood such as yucca or willow, was usually four to five feet long. Upon impact, the shaft would flex toward, and then spring away from, the prey leaving the stone-tipped foreshaft inside. The hunter would then retrieve the mainshaft and insert a new foreshaft. This weapon was particularly useful when hunting the mastodon and great bison, the earliest prey of its inventors.

Most of the "arrowheads" found today were used with the atlatl. The projectile points used with the bow and arrow, frequently called "bird points", were not used until approximately 700 A.D.

The picture on the left depicts an Indian using the atlatl. A copy of a Pecos River pictograph to the left of the central figure is that of a shaman with the atlatl in his right hand and several compound arrows in his left. To the right is a top view of a straight-style atlatl with leather finger loops; and details of the compound spear. At the far right are the Clovis and Folsom points. These are the oldest projectile points in the Americas, and date from 10,000 - 8,500 B.C. The oldest authenticated projectile point found at Enchanted Rock is a Plainview type, pictured above, dating from around 8,000 B.C.

whose influence was felt throughout the Plains. Although the excerpt is not specifically about Enchanted Rock or its native inhabitants, on a deeper level it speaks directly to the spirit of the place, Plains Indian spiritual leaders, and the mythological foundation of their religion. "[Wovoka was] by nature of a solitary and contemplative disposition, one of those born to see visions and hear still voices... His native valley, from which he has never wandered [was] roofed over by a cloudless sky in whose blue infinitude the mind instinctively seeks to penetrate to far off worlds beyond. Away to the south the view is closed in by the sacred mountain of the Paiute, where their Father gave them the first fire and taught them their few simple arts before leaving for his home in the upper regions of the Sun-land... It seems set apart from the great world to be the home of a dreamer."

THE IMAGINARY FRONTIER

Although the Spanish explorer Alvar Nuñez Cabeza de Vaca passed through Texas in the sixteenth century, possibly in the vicinity of the present location of Mason County, it would take another two hundred years before the Spanish would make their influence felt in the *Lomeria*, or Hill Country. In the 1700's several missions—Concepcion, San Jose, San Juan Capistrano and La Espada—were established in San Antonio. These missions soon became sanctuaries of the Lipan Apache, who were bitter enemies of the Comanche to the north.

The Spanish during this period were increasingly concerned about incursions into Texas by the French, who were supplying arms to the Comanche. In an effort to expand control of what the Spanish considered their territory to the north, they sent expeditionary forces into the Hill Country in search of a suitable site for a mission which was expected to serve several purposes. Apart from establishing an outpost in this unknown frontier, it would be the primary mission for converting the Lipan Apache to Christianity. The mission, with its Apache warriors, would also be a buffer against Comanche attacks further south, particularly on the settlement in San Antonio.

The area had been known as the Apacheria; however, the Comanche were rapidly claiming it as their own. In June 1753 an expedition was sent in search of a location for the proposed mission. Led by Lieutenant Juan Galvan from the Presidio de San Antonio de Bejar, the regions around the Pedernales and Llano Rivers were explored with disappointing results. Finally, along the San Saba River they found what they had been seeking; fertile soil, timber and abundant water.

The cautious Spanish sent another expedition to confirm the recommendation of Galvan. That expedition returned with even more intriguing information. Their Indian guides told stories regarding the *Cerro del Almagre*, or Hill of Red Ochre. Suddenly rumors abounded in San Antonio regarding the potential for gold and silver mines in the region.

Inspired by rumor, ten men with Lipan guides sought to locate the fabled Cerro del *Almagre* and their fortunes. But fortune turned against them when their guides deserted the expedition to join other Apache on an assault against the Comanche. The Apache were to rendezvous at a landmark called *La Rodilla*, or The Knee. In *Enchanted Rock Country*, Robert S. Weddle (1979), states: "in the account of the episode, however, occurs the only mention yet found in Spanish documents of a landmark that might be interpreted to mean Enchanted Rock... 'The Knee'... seems a fair description of the prominent feature."

On February 17, 1756, under orders from the governor of Texas, Jacinto de Barrios y Jauregui, Bernardo de Miranda y Flores departed San Antonio with twenty-three men with instructions to locate *Cerro del Almagre*. Eight days later, having endured torrential rains, flooded rivers, and rocky terrain, they arrived at the *Almagre*. Camping on Honey Creek, the expedition discovered a red ochre hill on Riley Mountain near the present-day Llano. Within the hill Miranda claimed to have found a tremendous stratum of silver-bearing ore.

Whether the *Almagre* is on Riley Mountian or Packsaddle Mountain is a matter of debate. Since Miranda never mentioned Packsaddle Mountain in his report some researchers have concluded that he was actually camped on that location. In the 20th Century abandoned mines, possibly Spanish, have been found in both locations.

"The mines which are in the Cerro del Almagre," Miranda reported, "are so numerous that I guarantee to give every settler in the province of Texas a full claim... The principal vein is more than two varas in width and in its westward lead appears to be of immeasurable thickness... I commanded that the work be continued on the cave of almagre, to which I gave the name and commanded that it be called San Jose del Alcazar. I also commanded that on the fol-lowing day six soldiers be furnished to explore for a long distance off to the west, as it was not feasible to continue the march to examine the other places, because most of the soldiers were now nearly on foot with the horses tired and footsore, and of those who accompanied me there was no one who was able to serve as a guide to discover the other Almagre Grande...

"Leaving [the camp of San Miguel toward the west, there are mineral veins again, although they are much scarcer than at San Joseph del Alcazar. I saw these for most to the ten leagues that I traveled until sighting the high hill they call Santiago."

Roderick Patten suggests in his article "Miranda's Inspection of Los Almagres: His Journal, Report and Petition," (1970) that *Cerro de Santiago* could well have been Enchanted Rock. Indeed its name comes as close in spirit to describing Enchanted Rock as *La Rodilla* does in describing its appearance.

We have no record, written or otherwise, for any Indian designation of Enchanted Rock. During the historic period most Native Americans spoke Spanish as a second language. *Cerro de Santiago* is Spanish for Hill of the Sacred One. Ending with an "o" makes "the sacred one" masculine, thus we can say, the "sacred man."

Among Native Americans anything sacred is said to have, or be, medicine. Thus, if we were to conjecture on the Indian name for Enchanted Rock we could surmise it was Hill of the Medicine Man, or Medicine Man Hill.

From a hill west of the *Almagre* (currently on Ranch Road 114) looking due south Enchanted Rock makes a unique and impressive sight.

Miranda returned to San Antonio three weeks later with ore samples which proved promising,

> *"The mines which are in the Cerro del Almagre," Miranda reported, "are so numerous that I guarantee to give every settler in the province of Texas a full claim... The principal vein is more than two varas in width and in its westward lead appears to be of immeasurable thickness..."*
>
> *--Bernardo de Miranda y Flores*

but skeptical officials and subsequent events worked against Miranda's discovery. Although the mine was never reopened, it gave birth to numerous legends of lost Spanish mines in the Central Mineral Region which persist to this day.

In 1756, the Mission Santa Cruz de San Saba was established on the banks of the San Saba River under the leadership of Father Alonso Giraldo de Terreros. Three miles upstream the Presidio de San Luis de las Amarillas was built to provide protection for the mission. But, as Robert S. Weddle points out in *The San Saba Mission* (1964), "While this placement reduced the likelihood of military meddling in mission affairs, it rendered impossible defense of the mission in case of attack."

The presidio was under the command of Colonel Don Diego Ortiz Parrilla, who considered the location of the mission ill-advised and almost immediately requested it be moved to the Rio de las Chanas (Llano River), where the fabled Cerro del Almagre would be close at hand. Parrilla's garrison was, at the time, the largest in Texas, with almost four hundred inhabitants, including women and children. Because the mission and its presidio was essentially Comanche territory, and because the Spanish were allies of the Apache, hostility was inevitable.

The mission was beset by problems too numerous to detail here. Perhaps Father Terreros said it all: "All Hell is joined together to impede this enterprise." Although the Apache had encouraged the establishment of a mission, they never lived up to their end of the bargain. Two months after the mission was founded, three thousand Apache arrived there but refused to stay. The Apache were on a mission of their own—enroute to either a buffalo hunt or a campaign against the Comanche, depending upon which chief one listened to. After receiving gifts from the Spanish, they departed returning a few days later with buffalo meat for the missionaries. But the Apache left again almost immediately. It seems certain the Apache knew that the enterprise, well inside Comanche territory, was doomed. But if it provided the pretext for an all-out conflict between the Spanish and the Comanche, so much the better; why fight an enemy when you can induce a superior force to take up the task? To further that end, the gifts the Apache accepted from the Spanish missionaries were left here and there on the trail in a effort to implicate the Spanish in the raids.

Seven months after being visited by the Spanish, Santa Cruz de San Saba was attacked by approximately two thousand Indians, many armed with French rifles. The Comanche, in association with the Tejas, Tonkawa, Bidai, and others, burned the mission to the ground. A few survivors escaped to the presidio, and after a brief siege the Indians abandoned the field of battle.

In 1766, Marquis de Rubi, the inspector general for King Charles III of Spain, was sent to Mexico to report on the condition and viability of the entire Spanish frontier. With the Spanish acquisition of Louisiana, the French threat to the Spanish claims on Texas ceased to be of concern. According to Rubi, the presidio on the San Saba defended an "imaginary frontier" and its men and material should be put to better use. The presidio was abandoned in 1768.

Despite Rubi's assessment, the frontier was real enough, as was the Comanche's ability to claim it for over a century. But the numerous legends of lost Spanish mines would prove irresistible to future settlers on the frontier and those legends would be Spain's most enduring legacy in the *Lomeria*, or Hill Country.

Even today, Enchanted Rock, Packsaddle Mountain, Riley Mountain, and the San Saba Mission inspire stories of lost treasure and abandoned mines. In effect, Rubi's imaginary frontier became the frontier for the imagination.

THE OTHER HISTORY

Smallpox Winter: 1839-1840

When writing historical accounts, cultural perspective is critical. When two cultures come into conflict over a piece of earth, "approved history" falls to the victor and becomes part of the spoils of war. Generally speaking, history is the mythology of the victorious.

Whether it is a brief history of Enchanted Rock, or the larger story of the "Winning of the West," the tendency is to focus on actual contact and conflict between the whites and the Indians. Consequently, it is possible to wrap an enormous tragedy into a simple sentence and move on. For a clearer picture we must turn to the Indian version of events.

Although it is generally assumed the Indians were a people without an official history, nothing could be further from the truth. Among the Plains Indians there were chronological records, or histories, dating back some two hundred years.

Known as *winter counts,* a single picture (or pictograph) was used to denote the most significant event of the year. These records, kept on buffalo robes, were used to aid memory when recounting the oral history of their respective tribes.

Among the Kiowa winter counts, from which the illustration for this article was taken, a picture above a black vertical bar was used to denote the winter count. The disease is indicated by red spots covering the figure of a man.

In 1885 James Mooney, a twenty-five-year-old former journalist began his fieldwork for the Bureau of American Ethnology. It is from his report, *Calendar History of the Kiowa Indians*, published in 1898 Mooney recorded detailed interpretations of their winter counts.

"This was the great smallpox epidemic which began on the upper Missouri in the summer of 1837 and swept the whole plains north and south, destroying probably a third, if not more, of the native inhabitants, some whole tribes being nearly exterminated... It appeared first among the Mandan about the middle of July, 1837, and practically destroyed that tribe, reducing them in a few weeks from about sixteen hundred to thirty-one souls.

"Their neighboring and allied tribes, the Arikara and Minitari, were reduced immediately after from about four thousand to about half that number ...

"From the Mandan it spread to the north and west among the Crows, Asiniboin, and Blackfeet. Among the last named it is estimated to have destroyed from six to eight thousand...

"In 1838 it reached the Pawnee, being communicated by some Dakota prisoners captured by them in the spring of that year. From the best information it seems probable that at least two thousand Pawnee perished, about double the whole population of the tribe today. It probably continued southward through the Osage until it reached the Kiowa and Comanche the next year, although it is possible that it may have come more directly from the east through the emigrating Chickasaw, who brought it with them to Indian Territory in the spring of 1838."

From Mooney's research the events of this period were more devastating to Native Americans than a hundred armed conflicts.

According to the Kiowa winter counts, the following year, 1839, a treaty of peace between the Arapaho and Cheyenne with the Kiowa, Comanche, and Apache was established.

GONE TO TEXAS

By the turn of the century the Spaniards faced a more immediate problem than the Comanche. The Mexican campaign for liberation had begun in 1810 and finally met with success in 1821.

With the Spanish out of the way, the Mexicans inherited the "Indian problem". Mexico's solution was to allow Anglos to settle that troublesome piece of land known as Texas. The Anglo settlers were to be a buffer between Mexico and the hostile Southern Plains Indian raiding parties which had been know to traverse the entire length of Texas, from north of the Red River down across the Rio Grande and into Mexico. With the Texans in the way, the Indians would get whatever they were after, or get killed, before reaching Mexico.

In 1822, with the blessing of the Mexican government, Stephen F. Austin, with three hundred families, founded San Felipe de Austin, forty miles west of present Houston. Immigrant Anglos poured into the area. Like a river that had exceeded it banks, the flood of dreamers, desperadoes, and the just plain destitute had left their lives in the States and had "gone to Texas".

Within eight years Austin's colony was home to over four thousand Texans. If the settlers had a hard time, at least they also had hope. The Indians were desperate. Epidemics of smallpox were devastating the Plains tribes from Canada to Mexico. Old hostilities between many tribes were set aside in their struggle for survival. There had been more tribes of Indians in Texas than in any other state, and those that still survived, roamed the Hill Country like dispossessed refugees. Although the Comanche dominated the region, they were intermingled with bands of Lipan Apache, Kiowa, Arapaho, Waco, Caddo, Tehuacanas, Cheyenne, Delaware, Shawnee, Cherokee and others.

As early as 1821, Austin had heard and repeated stories of a gold dust mine on the Llano River and an abandoned Spanish silver mine on the San Saba. In 1829, James Bowie and his brother Rezin, are said to have led a group of men searching for the Lost San Saba Mine. Some tales say they found the mine, others just the opposite.

In any event, the name 'Bowie' and '1829' carved on a stone pillar at the abandoned Presidio de San Saba, and the word 'mine', carved there later, added circumstantial substance to the tales.

With so many Indians on so little land coveted by so many Texans, and with legends of gold and silver in the region, trouble was a certainty. That same year, Captain Henry S. Brown led a group of thirty Texans on a campaign to subdue Waco and Techuacana Indians, who were tormenting Austin's colony. On their way to the headwaters of the Colorado they encountered hostile Indians twice, killing nine. The second encounter was at a place called 'the enchanted rock'. On his return Captain Brown described the landmark and is credited with having "discovered" Enchanted Rock.

One wonders whether Captain Brown and his men, having covered so much territory and encountered so few Indians, were hunting hostiles or, like the Bowie brothers, hunting treasure. If they hadn't heard of the legendary San Saba mine in 1829, which is unlikely, they would surely have learned of it two years later when Austin published a brief account of this fabled mine in a promotional booklet for his settlement.

The years that immediately followed were not suitable for such frivolous pursuits as searching for lost mines. The Texans, imported by the Mexicans as a buffer against the Indians, were bent on independence. Ironically, the Mexican government had gained independence and acquired Texas from Spain; and they lost that frontier a mere fifteen years later in 1836, when the Texans concluded their own war of independence.

With Mexico's interference out of the way, the attention of many Texans returned to the lost mines and the mysterious Enchanted Rock. In 1838 the *New York Mirror* published an account of a prospecting trip on the San Saba River that included mention of an "Enchanted" or "Holy Mountain" near the headwaters of Sandy Creek. According to the article, "The Comanche regarded this hill with religious veneration, and that Indian pilgrims frequently assemble from the remotest borders of the region to perform their Paynim [pagan] rites upon its summit."

In 1838 the general land office opened in Texas. Speculators and surveyors, intrigued by stories of lost gold and silver mines, began a concerted exploration of Indian lands, particularly in the vicinity of Enchanted Rock. For the Indians, it was nothing short of an invasion. Provided with arms and ammunition, both bought and stolen from the Mexicans, Indian attacks upon settlers and surveyors began to increase in frequency and ferocity. Surveyors, considered by the Indians as the advanced guard for settlers, were particularly at risk. During the first year after the land office was in operation, the majority of surveyors were killed in the line of duty.

Buffalo Hump's band then split up to evade capture, meeting later at the prominent landmark Enchanted Rock. After two years of captivity, Mrs. Webster managed to escape to San Antonio with her children. Upon her return, she told of gold and silver mines and brilliant stones the Indians possessed that looked like diamonds.

On March 16, 1838, a headright certificate issued to Anavato Martinez and his wife, Maria Jesusa Trevino, granted a league and labor of land which included Enchanted Rock. Given the seriousness of Indian troubles during that time, ownership of Enchanted Rock was largely wishful thinking.

During the summer of 1838, James Webster with his wife, children and a dozen hired hands, led his wagon train toward the fork of the San Gabriel River to settle his headright league. Enroute to their homestead they were attacked by a band of Comanches led by Chief Buffalo Hump. All the men were killed. Mrs. Webster, her young son, and three year old daughter were taken captive.

Buffalo Hump's band then split up to evade capture, meeting later at the prominent landmark Enchanted Rock. After two years of captivity, Mrs. Webster managed to escape to San Antonio with her children.

Upon her return, she told of gold and silver mines and brilliant stones the Indians possessed that looked like diamonds. The 'diamonds' were actually quartz crystals which were found in the area and were sacred objects to the Indians. Mrs. Webster's stories simply confirmed what the Texans already believed; there was gold, or at least silver, in the Texas hills.

In October of 1841, Anavato Martinez sold his headright certificate, which included Enchanted Rock, to James Robinson, who held title for three years before selling it to a business associate, Samuel A. Maverick.

JACK HAYS

"Me and Red Wing not afraid to go to hell together.
Captain Jack heap brave; not afraid to go to hell by himself."

—Chief Flacco, Lipan Apache guide

At the age of nineteen, Tennessean John (Jack) Coffee Hays emigrated to San Antonio in 1837, where he readily found employment in his profession as a surveyor. At the time the surveyors were also members of a ranging company, or as they were called at the time a spy company. These men were the only protection on the frontier and later came to be known as the Texas Rangers. Due to Hays' courage, leadership, and endurance, he rapidly rose to the rank of Captain. In those early days the Rangers who patrolled the frontier, lived like the Indians they fought; and a position of leadership among the Rangers was achieved only by the consent of the men. As Ranger Rip Ford wrote of Hays in 1885: "No officer ever possessed more completely the esteem, the confidence, and the love of his men."

Hays was an enigma. His boyish appearance and slight build—he was under five foot eight inches tall and weighed barely 150 pounds—belied his attributes as a leader of the hardiest and, of necessity, meanest men on the Texas frontier. Amid the other large and robust Rangers, Hays seemed more like a camp follower. Thin, pale, and restless, he spoke little and ate less. Yet when occasion demanded, Jack Hays could shoot straighter, fight meaner, ride faster, cuss fouler, yell louder and endure great hardships better than any man in his command.

J. W. Wilbarger, a Ranger serving under Hays, wrote in his book *Indian Depredation in Texas*, published in 1889: "Colonel Hays was especially fitted by nature for this frontier service. He was a man rather under the medium size, but wiry and active and gifted with such an iron constitution that he was able to undergo hardships and exposure without perceptible effect... I have frequently seen him sitting by his camp fire at night in some exposed locality, when rain was falling in torrents, or a cold norther with sleet or snow was whistling about his ears, apparently as unconscious of all discomfort as if he had been seated in some cozy room of a first class hotel; and this, perhaps, when all he had eaten for supper was a hand full of pecans or piece of hard tack. But above all, he was extremely cautious where the safety of his men was concerned, but when it was a mere question of personal danger his bravery bordered closely on rashness."

A year prior to Hays' arrival in Texas an event occurred in the Indian Queen Hotel in Washington, D. C. that would change the course of warfare against the Indians. There on February 25, 1836, twenty one year old Samuel Colt was examining with pride the patent he had just received for the Colt Paterson Revolving Pistol. Five years earlier, when Colt was a sailor aboard a ship bound for Calcutta, he whittled to while away the time, but he was no ordinary whittler. What he fashioned was his model for the weapon that would play a central role in the "winning of the West".

It is unclear when Colt came to Texas to promote his revolver, either in 1839 or 1840. Initially he was unable to find a market for his invention. Captain Hays, however, immediately recognizing the tactical advantage of the weapon, acquired several of the "five-shooters" for himself and his men. Hays and his Rangers, particularly Samuel Walker, tested the weapons and even recommended modifications, which Walker was sent back East to supervise.

In the hands of Jack Hays and his Rangers, the Colt revolver represented a sudden and decisive turn of events in confrontations with the Indian. Prior to acquiring the revolvers, the Rangers had to dismount in order to reload their muzzle-loading rifles, while the Indians, with their bows and arrows, could remain mounted and mobile.

Also, it was a common plan of attack for the Indians to draw fire and, while their opponent was reloading, to charge the defenseless adversary.

James Wilson Nichols, a scout in Hays' command, gives the following description of the training Hays demanded after the Rangers acquired the revolver: "We kept out scouts all the time, when one would come in another would go out, and those not on scout were every day practicing horsemanship and marksmanship. We put up a post about the size of a common man, then put up another about forty yards farther on. We would run our horses full speed and discharge our rifles at the first post, draw our pistols and fire at the second. At first there was some wild shooting but we had not practiced two months until there was not many men that would not put his balls in the center of the posts.

"Then we drew a ring about the size of a mans head and soon every man could put both his balls in the circle. We would practice this awhile, then try riding like the Comanche Indians. After practicing for three or four months we became so perfect that we would run our horses half or full speed and pick up a hat, a coat, a blanket, or rope, or even a silver dollar, stand up in the saddle, throw ourselves on the side of our horses with only a foot and a hand to be seen, and shoot our pistols under the horse's neck, rise up and reverse, etc."

In the fall of 1841 the twenty three year old Hays camped with his party of twenty Ranger surveyors on Crabapple Creek, not far from Enchanted Rock. Early the next morning a fellow Ranger, Ben McCullouch, overheard Hays talking to his guns—two of Colt's five-shooters. While giving them a good cleaning, Hays murmured; "I may not need you, but if I do I will need you mighty bad." A short time later Hays rode out alone to inspect the legendary Enchanted Rock.

Hays, thoroughly familiar with the Indian and their beliefs, must have known that if there were any Comanche in the area, they would not tolerate his intrusion on sacred land; furthermore, their reaction to a surveying party would be especially fierce. Needless to say, when the Comanche saw the notorious Jack Hays on their holy mountain with surveying equipment, they were as angry as teased wasps. When the Indians attacked, Hays headed for the summit, where he held out until his companions arrived to finish the fight.

The Comanche hadn't counted on Hays' Colts. With two five-shooters and a rifle he was better armed than ten men with muzzle-loading rifles. Especially when you take into account the element of surprise. The Comanche's old methods of attacking a stranded white where suddenly useless. According to most accounts, the Comanche lost between ten and twenty warriors in the confrontation. Out gunned and bewildered by the sudden change of events, the Comanche quit the field and sought escape in the labyrinth of Enchanted Rock Cave.

The credit for the victory went to Jack Hays, who couldn't resist the climb to the summit of Enchanted Rock, alone. But the truly unsung hero of the day was Samuel Colt.

Texas' most renowned Ranger, Hays attained the rank of Captain at twenty-three, major at twenty-five, and colonel at thirty-four. In 1849, the year of the gold rush, Hays left Texas for California. He served as sheriff of San Francisco County for four years, and in 1853, President Franklin Pierce appointed Hays Surveyor General of California. As part of his duties, Hays laid out the city of Oakland. It is said his last Indian fight was in Nevada in 1846. Jack Hays died in Piedmont, California, on April 25, 1883 at 75 years of age.

WILLIAM KENNEDY'S TEXAS

The groundwork for an accurate and comprehensive knowledge about Texas is found in the work of the Englishman Kennedy... It must be remembered, however, that the author ... had to rely upon reports of other persons, which caused errors and discrepancies to creep in."

–Dr. Ferdinand Roemer (1852)

Since the time of the Spanish, San Antonio had been the wellspring of legend regarding the Central Mineral Region. While many adventurers left San Antonio in search of lost Spanish mines, British diplomat Wiliam Kennedy visited San Antonio to mine the rich vein of tales regarding the mysterious frontier. Kennedy's book, *Texas*, published in 1841, was so well received in Germany it became the catalyst that shaped the destiny of the Texas frontier. Kennedy's descriptions of the "flower-spangled" landscape, lost mines, and the mysterious landmark Enchanted Rock fueled the imaginations of the German noblemen, who organized a society for Texas immigrants.

"Some specimens of gold and silver have been brought from the neighborhood of the San Saba hills and the mountainous region about one hundred and fifty miles northeast [sic] of Bexar," Kennedy wrote. Although Kennedy clearly noted his reliance on Mexican legend regarding the Spanish mines in the region the stories had the ring of truth.

Enchanted Rock, the most unusual landmark in the area and the gateway to the land of lost mines was described by Kennedy: "About twenty-five miles from the Colorado, on the northwestern branch of the Piedernales, is a rock, considered one of the natural curiosities of Texas. It is about two hundred feet high, of an oval form, and half embedded in the soil. It is composed of parti-colored flints, and reflects the sunbeams with great brilliancy. A spring gushing forth near its summit sprinkles its sides with water. Owing, it is supposed, to the presence of some phosphoric substance, it wears an illuminated aspect on dark nights. This rock is held sacred by the Indians, who visit it at stated periods, for the purpose of paying homage to the Great Spirit, after their wild and primitive fashion."

Despite the factual errors—there is no spring on its summit, it is composed of granite, not flint, and there is no phosphoric substance, etc.—nevertheless, the influence of Kennedy's work cannot be underestimated. It was the most comprehensive book on Texas written by a man who had a remarkable grasp on the political and economic issues of the time. In print, legend and rumor often carry the weight of fact, and many people of the day believed Kennedy's observations. And their belief determined their actions.

Consequently, Kennedy's book was instrumental in shaping the course of Texas history.

Kennedy's remarks regarding the presence of gold and silver mines were actually true. Shortly before the turn of the 20th Century Gail Borden, founder of the Borden Milk Company, owned a gold dust mine on Sandy Creek. Furthermore, silver mines have been in almost continuous operation in Llano County since Miranda's discovery in the 1700s.

THE NEW PROMISED LAND

There have been times when desperate people in hopeless situations were rescued by someone who arrives on the scene with the perfect combination of character, ability, and dedication. Such was the fortune of the German immigrants in Texas during the 1840's.

Baron Otfried Han Freiherr von Meusebach relinquished his hereditary title when he left Germany enroute to Texas. When he arrived in his new homeland in May 1845 he insisted on being known simply as John O. Meusebach. At the age of thirty three, having left family, friend, and title behind, he was to assume the almost impossible responsibility of commissioner general for the *Manizer Adelverein* for the Protection of German Immigrants in Texas.

Before leaving Germany Meusebach had devoted several years of study to the possibility of immigration, particularly to Texas. Of all materials written about the area, *Texas: The Rise, Progress, and Prospects of the Republic of Texas* (1841), by William Kennedy, British consul in Galveston was the most influential on Meusebach and the Society as well. Of particular interest to the Society was Kennedy's remarks on the existence of abandoned Spanish silver mines along the Texas frontier. Remarking on the book, Irene Marschall King, granddaughter of Meusebach, wrote in *John O. Meusebach: German Colonizer in Texas* (1967): "As an official Kennedy described places with exactitude and

authority. The very name of one landmark, Enchanted Rock, added to fascination the beckoning land. Meusebach hoped to probe for a scientific explanation of the mysterious sounds that were said to issue at times from the 640 acres of solid granite. He marveled that such an immense outcropping of mountainous rock was located in an area bearing the name "Llano" the Spanish word for "plain". He wanted to know the reason for this contradiction."

The Society was founded in March of the previous year by a group of German noblemen advocating immigration to Texas as a solution to the problems of political unrest and overpopulation facing Germany. The organization soon fell victim to the unscrupulous Texan, Henry Francis Fisher, when it purchased, sight unseen, an interest in the Fisher-Miller Land Grant. Located between the Llano and San Saba Rivers, the four million acre grant was in the very heartland of the legendary lost Spanish mines.

Fisher knew that the grant was too far from the coast and inhabited by too many Comanches to be suitable for a settlement. In order to make himself and his partner, Burchard Miller, seem important, Fisher claimed they had already put $60,000 into the project. But as Price Carl zu Solms-Braunfels, the first commissioner general, wrote in his report of the February 8, 1845 to the Society: "Yet every person here, from the President of Texas to the smallest Negro lad, knows that if Messrs. Fisher and Miller both were put under a cotton press, not one dollar, let alone $60,000 could be pressed out of them both." In a letter dated June 11, 1845, to his successor, Meusebach, the prince stated that Fisher was not worth "the cord it would take to hang him and Miller."

As if the swindle were not complete, Fisher obtained, in addition to the $11,000 for an interest in the grant, another $2,360 from the German's to purchase supplies for the settlers. Virtually all of the money was "misappropriated".

The Society's attempt to settle the grant was stalled in New Braunfels with 439 people waiting and, for the most part, living at the expense of the Society. Almost immediately upon assuming his responsibilities as commissioner general, Meusebach discovered, to his dismay, the Society was virtually bankrupt due to the financial mismanagement of the prince; and that the settlers, after a year of waiting to relocate to the grant, were understandably impatient. Added to those pressures was the fact that, according to the contract with the Republic of Texas, the grant had to be settled by August 1847. If not, all efforts and investments would have been in vain.

The fabled silver mines were the "ace-in-the-hole" for the Immigration Company. Solms-Braunfels mentions them in his book *Texas, 1844-1845*: "As to the knowledge of the mountains [the Fisher Miller Grant], most of it is obtained from the Mexicans, who in turn received it from the nomadic Indians. They describe the mountains as rich in ore, especially copper and silver. This statement is also confirmed by the old documents drawn up for the leasing of land. It is likewise well known that Texas as a territory had opened several silver mines, directed by the Spanish government; but immediately after the outbreak of the Mexican Revolution, due to the order of the government and to the inimical Indian tribes, these mines were destroyed. In spite of the many efforts, they have not as yet been found, nor are they likely to be, except by the establishing of colonies in the mountains. This can be done in time, provided there is sufficient protection against the Indians. Sojourns in the moutains up till now have been limited to four weeks because of the difficulty of carrying supplies such as biscuits, cornmeal, coffee, and bacon for approximately twenty men besides fodder for the beasts of burden."

Perhaps the Prince, viewed by many Texans as an effete primp, lacked the fortitude necessary for the task. Fortunately for the immigrants his replacement, Meusebach, was equal to the challenge.

With the deadline looming on the horizon, Meusebach pressed forward on the obligation to settle the frontier. In May 1846 he founded the community of Fredericksburg. In November Meusebach was informed in a letter from Germany written by the Executive Secretary of the Society that 4,304 immigrants were on their way to their new homeland in Texas.

If the prospect of even more immigrants wasn't enough to trouble Meusebach, Dr. Shubert, who was appointed by Meusebach as director of the settlement in Fredericksburg heaped on more problems. In Meusebach's own words from *Answer to Interrogatories* (1894) he wrote: "Without my knowledge and authorization the so-called "Doctor Schubert" had raised a company in the latter months of 1846 at Fredericksburg, and with his men and a cannon had started out to be the first one inside of the limits of the grant. He never dared to cross the Llano River, and cowardly returned without a shot fired, making now a report to me that it was impossible to get into the colony, because it was full of hostile Indians. That report could not be allowed to go abroad unrebuked. It would have created despondency amongst the emigrants and the Company..."

Meusebach began making plans to do the impossible— enter the land grant and attempt to treaty for peace with the Comanche. His assessment of the entire situation was clear: "With the buying of that grant the doom of the [immigration] company was sealed," Meusebach wrote. "They did not know what they bought. They undertook to fulfill what was impossible to fulfill. They did not have the means nor the time to fulfill it. Neither of the contracting parties nor their agents has ever seen a particle of the land in question. The territory set aside for settlement was more than three hundred miles from the coast, more than one hundred and fifty miles outside of all settlements, and in the undisturbed possession of hostile Indians. The government had promised no aid to take it out of the hands of the Indians. It had to be conquered," Meusebach concluded, "by

> *"A mob numbering about one hundred fifty persons," Roemer wrote, "armed with clubs and pistols came up the hill on which the buildings of the Verein stood. A deputation, composed of several individuals not enjoying the best reputation, went to the home of Herr von Meusebach. The rest contented themselves at first to wait for an answer from the delegation. When it was not forthcoming immediately, they crowded into the house and committed a number of excesses in the anteroom and uttered loud threats against the life of Herr von Meusebach. "*
>
> —Dr. Ferdinand von Roemer

force or by treaty."

At the request of the Prince Solms-Braunfels, the Berlin Academy of Sciences sent Dr. Ferdinand von Roemer to Texas in 1845 to evaluate the mineral assets of the grant. Upon his arrival in Galveston, Roemer met with William Kennedy before heading inland. Undoubtedly, the unusual geologic formation of Enchanted Rock, and the rumors of gold and silver mines Kennedy had included in his book were discussed with the geologist, particularly the Lost San Saba Mine which many believed to be located within the grant.

Roemer found the settlement in New Braunfels at the peak of insurrection. One the last day of December, 1846, "a mob numbering about one hundred fifty persons," Roemer wrote, "armed with clubs and pistols came up the hill on which the buildings of the Verein stood. A deputation, composed of several individuals not enjoying the best reputation, went to the home of Herr von Meusebach. The rest contented themselves at first to wait for an answer from the delegation. When it was not forthcoming immediately, they crowded into the house and com-

Meusebach pacified the rebels agreeing to several demands, one of which included his resignation as soon as a replacement could be found. Little did the mob realize that the very man they were planning to kill, or at least depose, was the only person in all of Germany and Texas who was capable of delivering to them all of their demands.

mitted a number of excesses in the anteroom and uttered loud threats against the life of Herr von Meusebach.

"In the meantime, the negotiations were carried on in the adjoining room. Mr. H. Fischer [sic], who had arrived from Houston a few days prior to this and from whom the Verein had bought the land, led the negotiations on the part of the deputation... The immediate motive for this insurrection was, however the machinations of a man, [Fisher] who to further his own selfish interests, was greatly concerned in getting rid of Herr von Meusebach..."

Meusebach pacified the rebels agreeing to several demands, one of which included his resignation as soon as a replacement could be found. Little did the mob realize that the very man they were planning to kill, or at least depose, was the only person in all of Germany and Texas who was capable of delivering to them all of their demands.

On January 14, 1847, a company of men led by Meusebach embarked on their journey to treaty for peace with the Comanche. Suffering ill health, Roemer had to wait to depart to Fredericksburg on January 20, arriving in Fredericksburg five days later.

On February 5, Indian agent Robert S. Neighbors arrived in Fredericksburg with an urgent message for Meusebach from the Texas Governor Pickney Henderson. The belated message urged Meusebach not to venture into Comanche territory for fear he would further arouse the already hostile Indians. Seizing the opportunity, Roemer joined Neighbors in pursuit of the Meusebach expedition.

"As my condition had improved in the meantime," Roemer wrote, "I resolved to make use of this opportunity to see the unknown Indian land on the Llano and San Saba rivers. My preparations were of the simplest kind and were completed within a few hours." With those somewhat offhand remarks, Roemer embarked on the adventure of a lifetime.

BRIEF HISTORICAL TIMELINE

- 12,000 B.C. -The first Americans arrive in Texas.
- 1753 -The first Spanish expedition in the area.
- 1756 -San Saba Mission established & destroyed.
- 1822 -Stephen F. Austin opens land grants.
- 1829 -Capt. Brown "discovers" Enchanted Rock.
- 1838 -Texas becomes an independent Republic..
- 1838 -General land office opens in Texas.
- 1838 -Anavato Martinez acquires Enchanted Rock.
- 1839 -Smallpox epidemic desimates native tribes.

- 1841 -Jack Hays' Indian battle at Enchanted Rock.
- 1841 -Sam Maverick purchases Enchanted Rock.
- 1845 -John Meusebach arrives from Germany.
- 1846 -John Meusebach establishes Fredericksburg.
- 1847 -John Meusebach & Comanche peace treaty.
- 1873 -Last Indian battle at Packsaddle Mountain.
- 1896 -Moss family acquires Enchanted Rock.
- 1927 -Enchanted Rock becomes a public park.
- 1978 -Enchanted Rock becomes a state park.

THE COMANCHE TREATY

The Treaty of Peace between John Meusebach and the Comanche Nation on March 1847 opened up almost four million acres for settlement. All or part of Concho, Kimble, Llano, Mason, McCulloch, Menard, Sansaba, Schleicher, Sutton, and Tom Green counties were created as a result of the treaty.

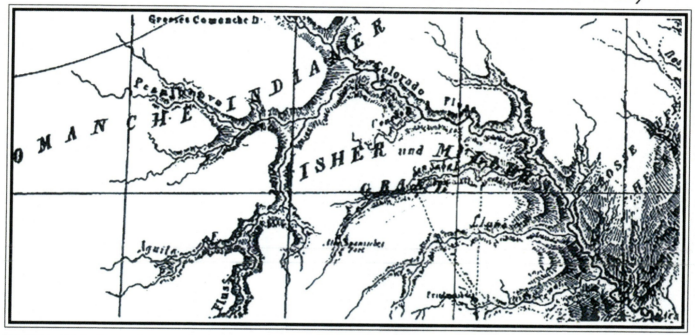

THE FISHER-MILLER GRANT: DETAIL FROM ROMER'S MAP CIRCA. 1847 SHOWING THE ROUND TRIP ROUTE INTO COMANCHE TERRITORY. THE MAP SHOWS THE COLORADO RIVER'S HEADWATERS TOO FAR TO THE SOUTH (BOTTOM LEFT).

The Meusebach expedition left Fredericksburg on January 22, 1847 to the Fisher-Miller grant which lay deep in the heart of Comanche territory. The group consisted of three wagons and forty men including Lorenzo de Rozas. As a child Rozas had been kidnapped by the Comanche. By virtue of his knowledge of the Comanche language and the territory, Rozas was appointed guide and interpreter. The German Immigration Company was virtually bankrupt and the desire to locate the Spanish silver mines was a faint ray of hope. The pragmatic Meusebach commented, "I do not really count the silver mines until we have them."

The expedition got off to an inauspicious start. On their second day, one of their men was seriously injured when his rifle exploded while on a buffalo hunt, so he had to return to Fredericksburg. Also, while building a campfire it began to burn out of control. In futility, Meusebach's men fought the prairie fire for thirty-six hours. The earth was burned for miles around and the event most certainly alerted any Indians in the area as to their presence.

Seventeen days after their departure Meusebach and his men encountered a hunting party of Shawnee in the immediate vicinity of the Llano River. After communicating to the Indians in broken English, they hired three Shawnee as hunt-

"I want to send men with that thing which red faces say steals the land [compass] and survey the entire region of the San Saba as well as the entire region as far as the Concho so that we will know the exact boundaries of the area where we can go and till the soil.

--John Meusebach speaking to the Comanche chiefs

ers who told Meusebach that his expedition was under constant surveillance by the Comanche whose tracks they had detected.

Finally, on February 5, the expedition encountered a party of Comanche advancing in their direction carrying a white flag. After assuring their leader, Ketemoczy, of the peaceful intent of the expedition the two parties joined in a meal. The next day, accompanied by even more Comanche, the Meusebach party was led to the main camp on the San Saba River.

The following account is from an anonymous report taken from the files of two officers of the expedition who later returned to Germany. Entitled "Meusebach's Expedition into the Territory of the Comanche Indians in January, 1847." It originally appeared in an early number of *Magazine of Literature From Abroad*: "The first day's journey beyond the Llano took us across large layers of granite, which could hold deposits of precious metals. The following day we crossed a

quartz region where we found rock crystals the size of a fist... On February 7 we finally approached their wigwams on the San Saba River and here we were given a ceremonious reception. From the distance we saw a large number of Indians in their colorful array coming down the hill in formation. As we came nearer they entered the valley, all mounted, and formed a long front. In the center was the flag; on the right wing were the warriors, divided in sections and each section had a chief, the left wing was formed by the women and children, also mounted. The entire spectacle presented a rich and colorful picture because the garb of the Comanche on festive occasions is indeed beautiful and in good taste. The neck and ears are decorated with pearls and shells and the arms with heavy brass rings. The long hair of the men is braided into long plaits, which, when interlaced with buffalo hair, reaches from head to foot and is decorated with many silver ornaments."

To complete this description of the Comanche, Jean Louis Berlandier wrote in his book, *The Indians of Texas in 1830*: "their skin is a fine copper-brown, heightened with cinnabar, of which they use a great deal. Some of them smear their bodies with powdered charcoal, others chalk, and many of them have three lines tattooed from the lower eyelid over the cheeks. The thing that makes the Comanche and several other natives look so different is the absence of beards, and the way they completely pluck out their eyebrows and lashes."

"As we approached the formation of the Comanche," the anonymous report continues, "it was requested of Mr. Meusebach that only he and few companions come nearer, and that was arranged. When our four or five men were within 100 paces, Lorenzo told us that if we fired our guns [into the air] as an indication of our confidence, that it would make a very favorable impression. This we did and the Comanche responded in a like manner. We were greeted with elaborate handshakes and then led into their village."

The Meusebach expedition of forty men discharged their guns in salute, thereby disarming themselves, while surrounded by two to six thousand Comanche [sources vary on the actual number]. That may have been a fool- hardy act. How- ever, in the face of such overwhelming numbers Meusebach's decision was not only the wisest, but possibly the only rational course of action.

Meanwhile, near Fredericksburg, In- dian agent Robert S. Neighbors, and ge- ologist Dr. Ferdinand von Roemer were enroute to over- take the Meusebach expedition. Neighbors car- ried an urgent message from Texas governor Henderson to call off the meeting for fear it would further incite the Co- manche. Roemer's mission, how- ever, was to inspect the mineral potential of the Fisher-Miller grant.

"We arose at sunup," Roemer recounted, " and after a short delay, caused by the preparation of our breakfast consisting of coffee, fried bacon and bread, our little company was on its way. Jim Shaw,

a six foot tall, strong Delaware chief, led the way on a beautiful American horse. Viewed from the rear, he looked quite civilized, since he wore a dark, stylish cloth coat which he had bought in Austin in a haberdashery, and a black semi-military oil cloth cap. Viewed from in front, his brown features, how- ever, betrayed his Indian origin immediately; and upon closer examination one found that his Euro- pean dress was by no means as complete as it ap- peared, for it lacked what is generally as- sumed to be a very essential part of a gentleman's dress, namely the trousers. Instead of these he wore deer- skin leggens, similar to our riding leggins, which reached half way up his thigh. Then fol- lowed Mr. Neighbors and I, with a young American whom Mr. Neighbors had en- gaged for the duration of the expedi- tion, and a common Shawnee Indian. Each of the two latter drove two pack mules which belonged to Mr. Neighbors and Jim Shaw."

On February 10 the group came upon the Meusebach expedition. "The three covered wagons which had been drawn into the center of the camp," Roemer wrote, "were an arresting sight in this pathless wilderness, in which up till now no wagon very likely had entered. Around these, the tents had been erected and in front of them whites and Indians mingled in a motley crowd. Even the whites were of diverse appear- ance and of mixed origin.

In addition to a number of un- affected Germans with genuine peasant features, one noticed in the immediate vicinity a group of Mexican muleteers with the unmistakable south- ern facial expression; then there were a num- ber of American surveyors, equally peculiar rep- resentatives of a third nationality, which von

> *"When my people have lived with you for some time, and when we know each other better, then it may happen that some wish to marry. Soon our warriors will learn your language. If they then wish to wed a girl of your tribe, I do not see any obstacle, and our people will be so much better friends... I do not disdain my red brethren because their skin is darker, and I do not think more of the white people because their complexion is lighter."*
>
> --John Meusebach speaking to the Comanche chiefs

Meusebach carried with him in order to point out to them the land to be surveyed."

While waiting for the Comanche chiefs to assemble at the camp on the San Saba River, Meusebach and Roemer received permission to lead an expedition to visit the old Spanish fort. In his accounts Roemer mentioned several times a "persistent rumor among the Texas settlers that the Spaniards had worked some silver mines in the vicinity of the fort." Upon arriving there, Roemer noted the names of previous visitors who had inscribed their names on the main portals: Padillo 1810, Cos 1829, Bowie 1829, Moore 1840.

After examining the area, Roemer concluded, "One may make the claim without hesitation, that at least in the vicinity of the fort no deposits of precious metals are present."

Meusebach's courage and his habit of walking among the Comanche unarmed earned the respect of the Indians. They even honored him with the name *El Sol Colorado*, or The Red Sun. Considering that the sun was the principal deity among the Comanche, the name had special significance.

Among the assembled chiefs were their three most prominent leaders: Santa Anna, Old Owl, and Buffalo Hump. Roemer, in his account of the meeting offered this description of the chiefs: "The three chiefs, who were at the head of all the bands of the Comanches roaming the frontiers of the settlements in Texas looked very dignified and grave. They differed much in appearance. [Old Owl] the political chief, was a small old man who in his dirty cotton jacket looked undistinguished and only his diplomatic crafty face marked him. The war chief, Santa Anna, presented an altogether different appearance. He was a powerfully built man with a benevolent and lively countenance. The third, Buffalo Hump, was the genuine, unadulterated picture of a North American Indian. Unlike the majority of his tribe, he scorned all European dress. The upper part of his body was naked. A buffalo hide was wound around his hips. Yellow copper rings decorated his arms and a string of beads hung from his neck. With his long, straight black hair hanging down, he sat there with the earnest (to the European almost apathetic) expression of countenance of the North American savage. He drew special attention to himself because in previous years he had distinguished himself for daring and bravery in many engagements with the Texans."

Meusebach's total lack of prejudice toward the Indians was in sharp contrast to that of Neighbors who believed all Indians were untrustworthy savages. After concluding a successful treaty of peace Neighbors attempted to take full credit for the agreement he had intended to prevent. In point of fact, had it been left to Neighbors, Meusebach would have been induced to turn back before attempting a treaty.

During the treaty Meusebach told the Comanche: "When my people have lived with you for some time, and when we know each other better, then it may happen that some wish to marry. Soon our warriors will learn your language. If they then wish to wed a girl of your tribe, I do not see any obstacle, and our people will be so much better friends... I do not disdain my red brethren because their skin is darker, and I do not think more of the white people because their complexion is lighter."

Most treaties between the whites and Indians

usually amounted to articles of surrender on the part of the latter. This was not the case with Meusebach's treaty. The whites and Indians were given equal recognition and dignity. The agreement was as if between two allies rather than two formerly warring factions. In exchange for three thousand dollars worth of presents, the Comanche agreed to allow the surveyors and settlers into the region without molestation. Also, the Indians could be allowed into German settlements and would "have no cause to fear, but shall go wherever they please." In exchange for Comanche protection from "bad Indians", it was agreed that "the Germans likewise promise to aid the Comanches against their enemies, should they be in danger of having their horses stolen or in any way to be injured."

Years later, Meusebach passed along the comments of Texas Ranger, Jack Hays as to the effectiveness of the treaty: "[Hays] was never molested nor lost any animals during his travel within the limits of our colony, but as soon as he passed the line he had losses."

"On March 3, we began our return trip to Fredericksburg," the anonymous report notes. "Scarcely had we completed a day's journey when a company of Comanches under Santana [Santa Anna] with their families joined us quite unceremoniously and informed us that they wished to accompany us all the way to Fredericksburg.

"Their company proved to be of some advantage to us, since they shot several wild horses. The meat was very appetizing. On March 5 we arrived at the Llano and on the 6th we camped on Sandy Creek near the noted Enchanted Rock. This mass of granite, so named because of its formation which have the appearance of monstrous giants and wild beasts, reminded us the castles along the Rhein. The Sandy Creek has a beautiful bed of granite, it's crystal clear water dashes from one shelf to another, forming many basins which are accessible by means of natural steps and offer an invitation for a bath. We found some bass in this beautiful water.

"On the following day, after a thirty five mile ride, we rejoiced when we reached Fredericksburg. It appeared to us even more cheerful because it happened to be Sunday and the settlers, arrayed

> *Most treaties between the whites and Indians usually amounted to articles of surrender on the part of the latter. This was not the case with Meusebach's treaty. The whites and Indians were given equal recognition and dignity. The agreement was as if between two allies rather than two formerly warring factions. In exchange for three thousand dollars worth of presents, the Comanche agreed to allow the surveyors and settlers into the region without molestation.*

in their colorful dress from the various districts of Germany, greeted us. They too, rejoiced when they saw us return at the head of and in peaceful association with a troop of Comanche Indians."

Although the Fisher-Miller grant contained 1,735,200 acres, the treaty included a total of 3,878,000 acres. In one day, just three months before the deadline to settle or forfeit the grant, Meusebach opened up what would become part or all of ten Texas counties. To call John Meusebach a man of intelligence, courage, tenacity, and vision would be an understatement.

In 1847, the Texas Rangers established a camp fourteen miles north of Enchanted Rock, under the leadership of Captain Samuel Highsmith. In *Recollections of Early Texas* Memoirs of John Holland Jenkins, the author and a member of the Highsmith company, wrote that Enchanted Rock was "a very remarkable freak of nature, being solid granite and covering an area of six hundred and forty acres of land."

He went on describe the landmark: "It is studded here and there with a kind of glittering material that resembles diamonds."

UTOPIA IN TEXAS

Among the first settlers in the Texas Hill Country were a group of German intellectuals, artists and musicians who were ill-prepared for frontier life.

The Texas frontier of the 1850s would seem an unlikely place to find communities with a passion for literature, phlosophy, music, and conversations in Latin. Just as unlikely would expectations be very high for communes in the Hill Country attempting to establish utopia along the Llano River.

But, in this area, the communities of Castell, Schoenburg, Bettina, and Leiningen were hotbeds for intellectual conversations and revolutionary social experimentation. These communities were the first to settle the Fisher-Miller Grant located between the Llano and San Saba Rivers.

Bettina, was named after the leading German feminist of her day, Bettina von Arnim.

Founded by Hermann Spiess and Dr. Ferdinand von Herff (a relative of John Meusebach). Using the watchwords "friendship, freedom, and equality," this colony was settled by a group of forty young men from Darmstadt, Germany. Called the Society of Forty, these early settlers were idealists who believed brotherly love and good will could replace civil law.

The community was supported for one year by the Society for the Protection of German Immigrants, after which their communal experiment was expected to sustain itself. Also called the "Darmstadters" as well as "The Forty," or the "Freethinkers" these intellectuals were ill prepared for the hard work of pioneer life. Shortly after their financial support ran out the community dissolved.

All of the utopian communities failed after a short period, and many of their families moved to, or helped settle, the community of Sisterdale, also known as the "Latin Settlement," and later, Boerne and Comfort. Of the first settlements in the Fisher-Miller Grant, only the community of Castell remains today; although after a severe flood the town was moved to the south bank of the Llano River.

In 1854 a New England journalist, Frederick Law Olmsted, entered Texas, made a tour of the state and recounted the events in, *A Journey Through Texas*. Enroute to New-Braunfels Olmsted met "a free-minded butcher" who "had ridden out early in the morning to kill and dress the hogs of one of the large farmers. He had finished his job and was returning [to New Braunfels]."

The butcher accompanied Olmsted and his party to New Braunfels. "It was sickly on the coast, but here it was very healthy. He [the butcher] had been as well here as he was in Germany—never had been ill. There were Catholics and Protestants among them; as for himself, he was no friend to priests, whether Catholic or Protestant. He had had enough of them in Germany. They could not tell him anything new, and he never went to any church."

Upon arriving in New Braunfels the butcher introduced Olmsted to Mr. Schmitz, owner of the Guadalupe Hotel. Olmsted was astonished by the quality of the accommodations. "There was nothing wanting; there was nothing too much, for one of those delightful little inns which the pedestrian who has tramped through the Rhine land will ever remember gratefully...

"We then spent an hour in conversation with the gentlemen who were in the room. They were all educated, cultivated, well-bred, respectful, kind, and affable men. All were natives of Germany, and had been living several years in Texas. Some of them were travelers, their homes being in other German settlements; some of them had resided long at Braunfels.

"It was so very agreeable to meet such men again, and the account they gave of the Germans in Texas was so interesting and gratifying, that we were unwilling to immediately continue our journey."

Later in his travels Olmsted found himself

> *"But he added that he would much rather educate them to be independent and self-reliant, able and willing to live by their own labor, than to have them ever feel themselves dependent on the favor of others. If he could secure them, here, minds free from prejudice, which would entirely disregard the conclusions of others in their own study of right and truth, and spirits which would sustain their individual conclusions without a thought of the consequences, he should be only thankful to the circumstances that exiled him.. "*
>
> —Frederick Law Olmsted

in Sisterdale, also known as the Latin Settlement, due to the desire of residents to make Latin their official language.

"Evening found us in the largest house of the settlement, and a furious norther suddenly rising, combined with the attractive reception we met to compel us to stay two days without moving...

"In speaking of his present circumstances, [the host] simply regretted that he could not give [his sons] all the advantages of education that he had himself had. But he added that he would much rather educate them to be independent and self-reliant, able and willing to live by their own labor, than to have them ever feel themselves dependent on the favor of others. If he could secure them, here, minds free from prejudice, which would entirely disregard the conclusions of others in their own study of right and truth, and spirits which would sustain their individual conclusions without a thought of the consequences, he should be only thankful to the circumstances that exiled him...

"After supper, there were numerous accessions of neighbors, and we passed a merry and most interesting evening. There was waltzing, to the tones of a fine piano, and music of the highest sort, classic and patriotic. The principal concerted pieces of Don Giovanni were given, and all parts well sustained. After the ladies had retired, the men had over the whole stock of student-songs, until all were young again. No city of fatherland, we thought, could show a better or more cheerful evening company. One of the party said to me: "I think, if one or two of the German tyrants I could mention, could look in upon us now, they would display some chagrin at our enjoyment, for there is hardly a gentleman in this company whom they have not condemned to death, or to imprisonment for life."

"I have never before so highly appreciated the value of a well-educated mind, as in observing how they were lifted above the mere accident of life... 'their mind to them a kingdom is,' in which they find exhaustless resources of enjoyment. I have been assured, I doubt not, with sincerity, by several of them, that never in Europe had they had so much satisfaction—so much intellectual enjoyment of life, as here."

The cultured, intellectual society of the Freethinkers was not without its attractions, especially to such an educated and informed person as John O. Meusebach, the founder of Fredericksburg.

According to Irene Marschall King, Meusebeach's granddaughter, John and his wife Agnes enjoyed their occasional visits to New Braunfels, "but a trip with her husband to the 'Latin Settlement' at Sisterdale was a stimulating experience. The men and women constituting the settlement were cultured and intelligent; so conversation was on an intellectual level. Merriment prevailed, too, and they enjoyed waltzing, and singing, and concert music on a fine piano. These Sisterdale settlers, self-constituted exiles from Germany, were not so successful in agriculture as in intellectual pursuits, but they had found their Arcadia in Texas and were content. Social and political freedom enabled them to make the most of life."

"After two years in the Sisterdale area, the five colonists [from Bettina] moved a little farther west and, in time, founded the town of Boerne, south of Sisterdale. In that settlement the Meusebachs found congenial friends. The same held for the settlement of Comfort, which was founded in 1854 by Ernst Altgelt. The Altgelt family and the Meusebachs were closely associated all their lives."

Meusebach shared with the Freethinkers a fondness for Latin. At his home in Loyal Valley he built a trellis-shaded structure for bathing out of native stone and cement with a fresh coating of whitewash. "When Meusebach would emerge from his frequent baths in this retreat," King wrote, "wearing a white shirt as was his custom, he would recite verses in Latin. '"Why in Latin?"' he was asked. His answer was, '"I speak gratitude to the Romans in their language for instituting a bath of this style, entered by steps."' Even Meusebach's tombstone carries the Latin inscription: *Tenax Propositi*—Texas Forever.

Although the utopian communities failed, the concepts of communes, cooperative communities, and back-to-the-earth movements loaded down with books would, a century later, create more conversation and debate than the German intellectuals of the Texas Hill Country could ever have imagined.

INTO THE MODERN ERA

*As the twentieth century approached Enchanted Rock
was becoming a recreational destination.
As responsible stewards on the land, the Moss family
is central to the closing chapter of the old ways
and the opening of the new.*

In 1845 Meusebach chose the valley of the Pedernales River for the settlement of Fredericksburg as it was half way between New Braunfels and the Fisher-Miller Grant. "Approaching the location within sight of the Pedernales River," Irene Marschall King wrote in *John O. Meusebach: German Colonizer in Texas,* "Meusebach halted his white horse to survey the land. It was a beautiful valley, with grass knee high and fine trees in abundance, especially along the river. As he came to the water's edge, he found a large pool, in which fish and soft-shelled turtles abounded. A short distance downstream the water cut through high banks to a ten-foot-high waterfall, which spread into a crystal-clear basin. At one point the river was one hundred feet wide, Grapevines festooned high in the trees..." King continues, "The countryside was covered with abundant pasture grasses, with deep humus underneath, which would produce excellent farm products... Meusebach visualized sugar, indigo, and tobacco crops, noting that the climate was favorable for fruit growing and for horticultural experiments. The native grapes could be used as rootstock for improved varieties. Meusebach's father had previously sent cuttings to be used for grafting."

Today the Perdernales River Valley, with its peach orchards and vineyards attest to Meusebach's clear-sighted, if not prophetic, assessment of the area as one favorable for fruit growing and vineyards. The abundance wildflowers in the area continues to be one of the major seasonal attractions in Texas.

The Pedernales River Valley has become a destination in itself offering quality lodging, fine restaurants, diverse shopping, award-winning wineries, live music venues, nearby state and national parks plus some of the best sightseeing in the state of Texas.

Discovery of gold in California in 1849 precipitated a rush of emigrants seeking their fortune. Fredericksburg became the last supply stop for the forty niners until they reached Hueco Tanks located near El Paso. A member of one of the wagon trains, C. C. Cox, was assigned to hunt game for the group. Upon reaching Enchanted Rock, though not mentioning it by name, he said it was a granite hill some "two hundred feet high". Cox noticed a hollow sound beneath the granite caused by his horse's hooves.

"The surface of the mound had the appearance of petrified sand," and Cox attempted to break through into what he imagined would be a large cavern beneath. He finally abandoned the task once he realized there was no cave, but only a small hollow hear the surface.

Special mention should be made of an individual who was most likely Enchanted Rock's most permanent resident. Rafe Maner, an emancipated slave was born in a log cabin between the base of the Rock and Sandy Creek in 1850. He lived in the cabin until his death in 1920.

The cabin was later moved across the creek where, some years later his birthplace was demolished.

The last recorded conflict between Indians and whites in the Hill Country occurred in 1873. Known as the Fight on Packsaddle Mountain, it was precipitated when a cow on the Moss ranch (in what is now Llano County) came into the ranch house with an arrow sticking out of its side. A party of eight ranchers, including W. B. Moss and his two brothers, was raised to pursue the Indians. They found approximately twenty one Indians encamped on Packsaddle Mountain. In the ensuing fight at least three Indians, probably Apache, were killed and three of the ranchers wounded. So closed the last account of Indian warfare in the region. With the lands surveyed, and settlements springing all along the frontier, the Indian tribes were rapidly becoming a relic of the past. Many of these settlers found their fortunes not in gold, but cattle.

In October of 1841, Anavato Martinez sold his headright certificate, which included Enchanted Rock, to James Robinson, who held title of the property for three years before selling it to a business associate, Samuel A. Maverick. The term *maverick* comes from this man. As stray cattle were plentiful in Texas, Maverick refused to brand his cattle. Consequently, any unbranded cattle were said to be Maverick's. The term was later expanded to include any person who acts independently.

Maverick really wasn't a cattleman, but essentially an entrepreneur, who bought Enchanted Rock, speculating on its potential for mineral wealth. When Maverick's widow sold the property around 1880 to N. P. P. Browne, she retained all the mineral rights. In 1886, Enchanted Rock was purchased by John R. Moss, who sold it in less than a year to J. D. Slaytor, and C. T. and A. F. Moss.

In 1896 the Moss family bought out Slator's interest, which was inherited by Tate Moss in 1927. Albert Faltin purchased Enchanted Rock in 1946, selling an undivided half interest to Charles H. Moss the following year. For decades afterward the Moss family continued the tradition of operating Enchanted Rock as a private park.

As the twentieth century approached Enchanted Rock was becoming a recreational destination. The Moss family is central to the closing chapter of the old ways and the opening of the new.

Although ownership of Enchanted Rock changed hands frequently, a constant throughout the twentieth century has been its use as parkland. At the outset of this century Enchanted Rock was frequently open to the public for picnics, dances, parties, and numerous other events, including religious services held on its summit by the Reverend Dan Moore ("On this rock I will build my church.").

Enchanted Rock officially opened to the general public as a privately operated park on June 22, 1927. The event was celebrated by thousands of visitors, including Governor Dan Moody, who dedicated Enchanted Rock as "Texas most wonderful summer resort." The highlight of the day, however, occurred when a celebrant named

Bradshaw drove his brand new Pontiac to the summit. This was not the only roadtrip up Enchanted Rock. A local Chevrolet dealer in Llano occasionally used the massive dome to demonstrate the performance of his autos.

Finally, in 1978 the Moss family decided to sell Enchanted Rock and diverse offers came in—from granite quarry operations to a Dallas developer who planned to build high dollar townhouses.

Another offer came from Lincoln Borglum who proposed using Enchanted Rock to sculpt a monument in honor of Texas heroes in the spirit of Stone Mountain with its Confederate heros, or to Mt. Rushmore. Lincoln, the son of Gutzon Borglum who designed Mt. Rushmore, is credited for completing his fathers work.

It is to the everlasting credit of Charles and Ruth Moss that they decided to reject those offers in favor of an offer from the Nature Conservancy in 1978. That organization held title for Enchanted Rock until the Texas Parks and Wildlife Department could allocate funds to purchase the tract a month later. Enchanted Rock was accepted on the National Registry of Archaeological Sites on August 24, 1984.

So it was that this ancient sacred landmark became one of the state's most remarkable natural & cultural treasures, attracting over 350,000 visitors annually.

Some come to here to rock climb, some to picnic or camp out. Still others are on a pilgrimage, seeking to connect with the spirit of Enchanted Rock, and by doing so rekindle their spirit within.

Enchanted Rock State Natural Area is located 16 miles north of Fredericksburg on Ranch Road 965. From Llano take Texas 16 South 16 miles, turn right on Ranch road 965. Enchanted Rock is 8 miles to the south.

Opened year round, the park offers 46 tent sites for overnight campers with tentpads, picnic tables, overhead shelters, barbecue pits, and fire rings. An attractive playground and modern rest room facilities complete with solar-heated showers are available to walk-in campers.

For the more adventurous back packers, the park has three remote camping areas and each of the remote areas is equipped with composting toilets.

There are 63 picnic tables, a playground and restrooms located in the area provided for day visitors. Campers should make reservations two to three months in advance.

Day visitors should arrive early—before noon—as the park frequently fills up and parking is unavailable until after 4:30 or 5 p.m. For more information including all entry fees phone 830-685-3636.

LEGEND AND FACT

Did the Indians at Enchanted Rock really practice human sacrifice to an angry god as many legends tell us?
To find the answers to these questions we have to look in the right places and ask the right questions.

There are many unusual stories regarding Enchanted Rock. In the absence of fact, legend and speculation combined to answer compelling questions. In the past, such stories have been the only source of readily available information on Enchanted Rock. The stereotype of the Indians as superstitious savages motivated by fear and ignorance was at the heart of these tales.

It is often said that the Indians feared Enchanted Rock, that they would not even shoot arrows in its direction. In fact, it was not fear but respect, that motivated their actions. The Indians held Enchanted Rock as a sacred, living entity. Who among us would discharge a gun in a church, temple, or synagogue? And if we refused to do so, who among us would truthfully say fear motivated our actions?

Another common tale is that the Indians were afraid of the Rock because of the mysterious "groaning" sounds it emanated. Contemporary geologists attribute this phenomenon to the rapid contraction and expansion of granite during sudden changes in temperature.

Despite such logic, if those sounds do occur, would not the entire granitic region in Gillespie, Llano, Burnet, and San Saba Counties have been feared or held sacred by the Indians?

Also, if the Indians feared Enchanted Rock, why are there so many ancient campsites so close to the place? There are, in fact, archeological sites on both sides of Sandy Creek, upstream and downstream for miles.

Several tales of Indians sacrificing virgins or other members of their tribe at Enchanted Rock to appease an "angry god" have been circulating for years. However, in the Plains Indian cultures there is no evidence that they ever practiced human sacrifice of their own tribal members to appease the Great Spirit, or any other deity. What we do find, due to a drastic reduction in their numbers to disease and conflict with Whites, is a tradition of tribes capturing women of other races in order to bear children and increase their numbers.

The tales of intertribal sacrifice may well have their roots in earlier contacts between the Spanish and Aztec cultures which were handed down from conqueror to conqueror. As Peter Furth noted in Man's rise to Civilization, "Human sacrifice never occurs in societies beneath the level of chiefdom... Only as societies become increasingly complex does the awareness of kinship lessen; only then does man become inclined to sacrifice one of his own kind or any animal surrogate." Other studies have suggested that human sacrifice is found in large communities of early agrarian cultures; not among hunter-gatherer cultures.

There is another story of a white woman who escaped her Indian captors, only to spend the balance of her life in total madness at Enchanted Rock. Her howls, it is said, created fear among the Indians. This story actually has a ring to truth. The only problem is, again, the emphasis on fear, which is inappropriate when applied to an entire race. Actually, the Plains Indians considered the insane as having been touched by the Great Spirit. The insane were respected, avoided, sometimes cared for, but never molested.

These and similar stories have been circulating for generations and will doubtless continue. Setting these legends aside, there is still enough inherent magic and mystery regarding Enchanted

> *"Human sacrifice never occurs in societies beneath the level of chiefdom... Only as societies become increasingly complex does the awareness of kinship lessen; only then does man become inclined to sacrifice one of his own kind or any animal surrogate."*
>
> —Peter Furth, Mans Rise to Civilization

Rock to satisfy even the most unimaginative mind. There are numerous contemporary stories of people—of all ages and from all walks of life—who have seen spirits of vanished Indians and heard the sounds of ancient drums.

A particularly interesting account is found in *Legends of Texas Rivers and Sagas of the Lone Star State* by Fannie May Barbee Hughs, published in 1937. In the chapter entitled "The Legend of Enchanted Rock" the author writes, "Near the head of the Perdernales is the 'Enchanted Rock'. Little is known of this singular rock, but legend has it that it is supernaturally illuminated. It is accessible by means of a natural stair which winds around it to the top.

"As one approaches, an aureole, ghostlike in appearance, envelops him, and as he steps on the stairs the rock begins a circular movement and the traveler's ears are filled with incredible and peculiar sounds. These sounds challenge investigation."

While this story has little basis in fact it does illustrate how folklore and personal experience blend and find their way into history.

The Indians believe the mountain spirits live, that their profound message can still be heard today. The stories of humans can be lost, but the spirit of the mountain lives forever. Its voice is as ancient as The Enchanted Rock.

On Sacred Ground

*Did the Native Americans really fear Enchanted Rock?
If not, how do we explain the many stories
handed down to us making such claims?*

The Sweat Lodge (without covering), based on a photograph by Marianne Greenwood.

Of all the stories currently in print regarding Enchanted Rock, the most often repeated goes something like this: "The Indians feared Enchanted Rock and the evil spirits which they believed dwelled there. Consequently, early settlers frequently found safety and refuge on its summit from the pursuit of indians."

These stories, which didn't appear in print until the 1900s, have been repeated so often they are accepted by newspaper and magazine editors today without question. However, such notions are far from the truth and reveal, if nothing else, a widespread ignorance regarding the traditional beliefs of Native Americans.

Enchanted Rock was considered sacred ground among the Indians of Texas. All historical accounts from the Spanish of the 1700s and the Texans of the 1800s have established this fact. None of those accounts mention "evil spirits."

According to the Apache, the Giver of Life saw the lives of The People were in disarray and the social fabric degenerating, so He sent the Gahn spirits from the four corners of the Earth to the summit of the sacred mountain to teach The People a better way to live.

The Kiowa believed that the Great Spirit sent Gahe, the spirit of the mountain, to give guidance and consolation to their people; Gahe, they believe, lives forever in the mountain's caves. The Comanche, and other Plains tribes would go to the summit of the sacred mountain seeking a vision from the Great Spirit to inspire and teach them the deeper secrets of their path in life. None of these traditions refer to evil spirits haunting the sacred mountain. What we do find, that speaks directly to the Indian's reluctance to pursue the early pioneers to the summit of Enchanted Rock is the tradition of the sweat lodge ceremony. Believed by some to be the most ancient of all Indian rites it employs those universal elements of earth, air, fire, and water. This ritual, it should be understood, precedes both the Gan ceremony and the vision quest.

The basic structure of the sweat lodge is simple: a small dome is built of willow branches; in the center of the lodge frame a pit is dug which will later hold the heated rocks for the ceremony. The dirt from the pit is used to make a path from the entrance (which faces East or West depending on tradition) to a mound or altar at the end of the path; just beyond that a firepit is constructed which will heat the rocks.

The dome is covered with hides, tarps, or any material which will keep the lodge airtight. A covering for the entrance is made from the same material. Once the stones are heated the participants enter the lodge, either naked or with loincloths. The stones are brought in, a few at a time. Water is poured over the stones and the resulting steam creates the sweat bath which, on the physical level, removes toxins from the body. If nothing else, Western traditions can accept this aspect of the ritual as fact.

Anyone familiar with the tradition may cringe at this oversimplification. It can be said without exaggeration that Native Americans are profoundly spiritual—even their ceremonies are preceded with ceremonies. Actually, every aspect of the sweat lodge ritual, beginning with the construction of the lodge involves specific prayers, a specified number of willow branches, rocks, and so fourth, all symbolically signifying certain aspects of their ancient traditions. Even the fire to heat the rocks is traditionally constructed with a given number of logs placed in precise alignment to the cardinal directions. Like many Indian rituals, what seems very simple, or even simplistic, is actually profoundly rich in metaphor and meaning.

With prayer and song they endure discomfort, often in the extreme, suffering for their faith. In total darkness time and space dissolve. Then, at a point which sometimes seems just this side of eternity, they emerge from the lodge. Weak and wobbly from the experience, crawling like precocious newborns from the womb of mother earth, they emerge, cleansed.

Every act, every object involved in the ceremony, creates an inner-connected web between form and function, physical and metaphysical, to produce a spiritual transformation in the individual.

On the earthen floor covered with sage-the sacred herb-the participants sit around the metaphorical center of the universe. With prayer and song they endure discomfort, often in the extreme, suffering for their faith. In total darkness time and space dissolve.

Then, at a point which sometimes seems just this side of eternity, they emerge from the lodge. Weak and wobbly from the experience, crawling like precocious newborns from the womb of mother earth, they emerge, cleansed.

Through this ceremony that is at once an act of purification and absolution, the participants stand at the threshold between spirit and matter. Only then are they worthy to ascend the heights to the summit of the sacred mountain.

BEDROCK METATES Mano, Matate & Mythology

*Frequently located at campsites near streams or springs
the concave depressions in the bedrock were used for grinding seeds.
These matates are constant reminders of an ancient past.*

Bedrock metates are one of the few Indian artifacts on view at Enchanted Rock State Natural Area. The metate and its companion piece, the mano, compromise a two-part tool used for grinding seeds and beans in the preparation of food These are the earliest "flour mills." In this region they often ground mesquite beans which were used in the preparation of a kind of bread.

The metate is a stationary, concave, slab of stone upon which the food is placed to be ground.

The mano, generally slightly larger than fist size, is then placed on top of the material to be processed, and applying a grinding motion, the seeds, beans, or nuts are then pulverized into the consistency of flour.

In use by Native Americans for over 10,000 years, the term metate is derived from the Aztec word metlatl; and mano (which means "hand" in Spanish) is a corruption of the Aztec word Metlapil, which, literally means "son of the metate."

Taken together, these inseparable tools can be viewed as sculptures of deities. The Mother (*metlatl* or metate), and the Son (*metlapil* or mano) are comparable to numerous "Madonna and Child" symbols from other cultures.

In each case the Mother is the throne. In her lap is cradled the Divine Son — the redeemer of life and culture. We can add to this image the plant *teosinte*, (pronounced "tA-O-'sin-tE")an Aztec word meaning "God's grass," which researchers believe

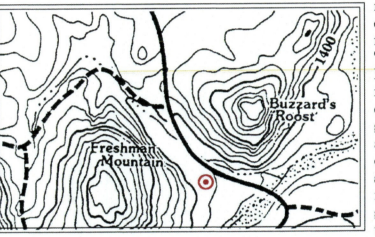

was corn's wild ancestor. Teosinte is a small single row cob of corn about 1.5 inches long consisting of some 5 to 12 kernels. Corn had been considered a deity among the many native tribes in Central and North America.

Between the sacred mother and divine child a life-giving sacrament was prepared. The bedrock metates at Enchanted Rock are identified by the concave depressions on granite boulders which are, as a result of years of use, polished smooth. There are numerous depressions in granite, however, if they are not smooth to the touch they are not metates.

Bedrock metates are found in association with campsites. Remember, it is illegal to collect any material from Enchanted Rock. The fine pieces of flint generally found in association with campsites are called "lithic scatter." These are not to be collected as doing so will destroy the larger artifact which is the campsite itself.

The map shown here indicates the general location of the bedrock metates which are to be found near the trail in a small stand of live oak.

Other bedrock metates have been located at numerous locations in the Enchanted Rock area, particularly along the tributaries leading into Sandy Creek. As the manufacture of metates and manos require considerable work, bedrock metates are evidence that these sites were favored campsite of the Native Americans.

Take only pictures. Leave only footprints.

AFTERWORD

Enchanted Rock took a firm hold on me from the moment of my first encounter in 1962. At the time, the only information on the place was a booklet, *Facts and Fiction about the Enchanted Rock*, by Charles Moss, who owned and operated Enchanted Rock as a public park until its sale to the Nature Conservancy in 1978.

Although the Moss booklet preserved the legends and folk tales of Enchanted Rock, there was nothing in print on the history of this remarkable landmark. The knowledge I held of my own Native American heritage told me that many of the legends, especially those regarding the Native Americans' fear of The Rock and allegations that they practiced human sacrifice, had no basis in fact.

In 1980, I decided to become an expert on Enchanted Rock and provide a more accurate version of this sacred landmark. "How hard can that be?" I asked myself. At the time I didn't realize that I would have to do some serious research in a variety of fields to acquire a truer understanding of the topic.

All of my research failed to open the door to the very essence of the sacred nature of The Rock. Then, in 1987, as a journalist for *The Highlander* newspaper in Marble Falls, I was assigned to cover an event at Enchanted Rock—The Harmonic Convergence. [See: www.texfiles.com/enchantedrocktexas/harmonic-convergence/preface.htm]

While there I was drawn into a deep mythological realm.

On my return home, for the first time, I prayed for guidance before writing an article. I pulled book after book from my library and they practically opened themselves to the appropriate passages. As I wrote, I seemed to understand more than I knew. It was as if all the tumblers had fallen into place and unlocked an understanding of the true nature of Enchanted Rock and its significance as a sacred site. From that moment, the rather pedestrian history I was writing took on a deeper meaning and wider scope.

Eventually, in 1990, I was to live on the XLN Ranch adjacent to Enchanted Rock State Natural Area. That place provided the inspiration I needed to pull together the volumes of research I had acquired along with my early drafts and my new understand of mythology and sacred geography.

The project seemed endless. At some point I had to tell myself, "enough is enough" and pull it all together. Finally.

I want to leave something of my love and understanding of Enchanted Rock behind, regarding its history, legends, desperados and dreamers. I've taken The Rock as it is and for what it was, and I've tried to hold on to that long enough to harness some of its spirit between the covers of this book. I know if I wait much longer it could be too late. This voice will not last forever.